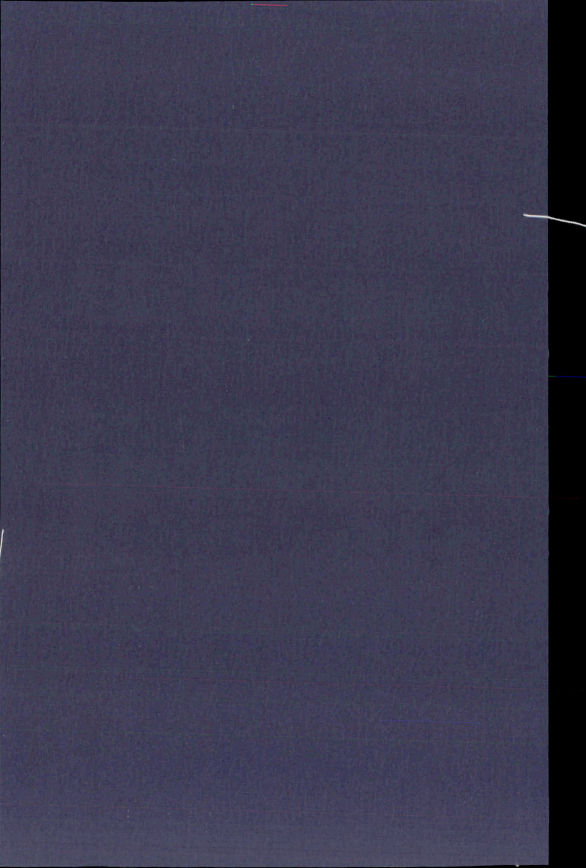

SNAPSHOTS IN HISTORY

THE COLLAPSE OF THE SOVIET UNION

The End of an Empire

by Andrew Langley

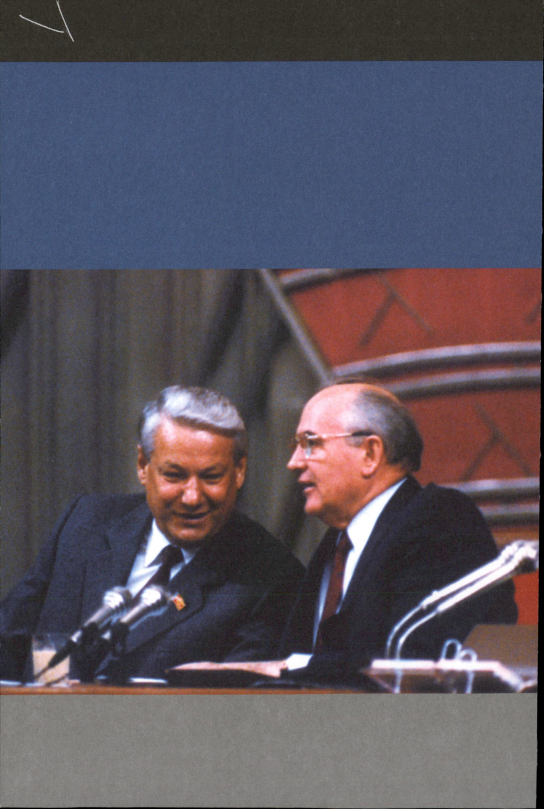

THE COLLAPSE OF THE SOVIET UNION

The End of an Empire

by Andrew Langley

Content Adviser: Derek Shouba, Adjunct History Professor
and Assistant Provost, Roosevelt University

Reading Adviser: Katie Van Sluys, Ph.D.,
School of Education, DePaul University

COMPASS POINT BOOKS

MINNEAPOLIS, MINNESOTA

Compass Point Books

3109 West 50th Street, #115
Minneapolis, MN 55410

Visit Compass Point Books on the Internet at
www.compasspointbooks.com
or e-mail your request to
custserv@compasspointbooks.com

For Compass Point Books
Jennifer VanVoorst, Jaime Martens, XNR Productions, Inc.,
Catherine Neitge, Keith Griffin, and Carol Jones

Produced by White-Thomson Publishing Ltd.

For White-Thomson Publishing
Stephen White-Thomson, Susan Crean, Amy Sparks,
Tinstar Design Ltd., Derek Shouba, Peggy Bresnick Kendler,
Laurel Haines, and Timothy Griffin

Library of Congress Cataloging-in-Publication Data
Langley, Andrew.
 The Collapse of the Soviet Union : the end of an empire /
 by Andrew Langley.
     p. cm. — (Snapshots in history)
 Includes bibliographical references and index.

 ISBN-13: 978-0-7565-2009-0 (hardcover)
 ISBN-10: 0-7565-2009-6 (hardcover)

1. Soviet Union—History–Juvenile literature. 2. Gorbachev, Mikhail
Sergeevich, 1931– Juvenile literature. 3. Yeltsin, Boris Nikolayevich, 1931–
Juvenile literature. 4. Post-communism—Juvenile literature. I. Title.
 DK266.L315 2006
 947.085′4—dc22   2006003003

THE COLLAPSE OF THE SOVIET UNION

Contents

The Coup that Failed

Chapter

1

It was late afternoon on August 18, 1991. Mikhail Gorbachev, president of the Soviet Union, was sitting in the study of his *dacha*, or country house. He had come to this peaceful villa, surrounded by peach orchards on the shores of the Black Sea, with his wife, daughter, son-in-law, and grandchildren.

He was supposed to be on vacation. Moscow, the Soviet capital, with all its problems and demands, was far away. Every day, Gorbachev and his wife, Raisa, took long walks in the lovely countryside. However, there was an important speech to write and other state matters to attend to, so now he was hard at work at his desk.

At 5 P.M., his chief guard came in. The guard told Gorbachev that a group of senior government officials had arrived to see him. Among them were powerful figures such as Yuri Plekhanov, head of the KGB , the Soviet secret police. Gorbachev was surprised and annoyed, because he was not expecting any visitors. Worse still, he had given orders that no one was allowed onto the grounds of the dacha without his consent.

Gorbachev was on vacation at his country house overlooking the Black Sea during the 1991 coup.

He picked up the telephone to find out what was happening. All five of the phone lines were dead. Gorbachev realized that something sinister was happening and told his family that he expected trouble. After a long wait, the visiting officials were shown into the study. They told Gorbachev that the Soviet Union was sliding into disaster and that the State Emergency Committee had taken charge.

They said that the State Emergency Committee did not like the way the president was running the country. For more than 70 years, the vast collection of states called the Soviet Union had been ruled rigidly by the Communist Party. But Gorbachev had started a program of sweeping reform, which was changing the whole system. The committee feared that this change would lead to the breakup of the Soviet Union—and with it an end to Communist Party control.

The visitors said that the State Emergency Committee would restore order in the land. They told Gorbachev that he must declare a state of

---

THE SOVIET UNION

The Soviet Union, or Union of Soviet Socialist Republics (U.S.S.R.), was established in 1922 and eventually became one of the most powerful countries on Earth. The U.S.S.R. was made up of 15 national republics in Eastern Europe and Northern Asia. Among these republics were Ukraine, Belarus, Georgia, Lithuania, Uzbekistan, and Kazakhstan, but by far the biggest and strongest was Russia. Moscow, the capital city of the U.S.S.R., was in Russia, and the main language was Russian. There was only one political party, the Communist Party, which had total power.

emergency. Then, he would have to sign a decree handing over his powers to Vice President Gennady Yanayev. They had brought all the documents with them. Gorbachev was outraged. He later wrote: "I had promoted all of these people—and now they were betraying me!"

Gorbachev had dedicated his life to reforming and modernizing the Soviet Union. These men wanted to go back to the "bad old days" when the state controlled everything. Defiantly, he refused all of their demands. They told him to resign. At this, he lost his temper, swearing at the plotters and telling them they were all criminals.

The men left, but Gorbachev and his family were still in a very dangerous position. They were prisoners inside the house and its grounds, which were surrounded by two lines of KGB guards. Warships patrolled the Black Sea nearby. Communication with the outside world by telephone or television had been cut off. The only news of what was happening came through Raisa's tiny portable radio.

Nearly 700 miles (1,120 kilometers) away in Moscow, plenty was happening. The State Emergency Committee was already moving to seize power. Early the next morning, tanks rumbled through the streets of Moscow to guard key positions.

The plotters announced that there was a state of emergency. They promised to safeguard the

11

country against "the chaos and anarchy that threatened the life and security of citizens of the Soviet Union." They said that President Gorbachev was sick and that the vice president would take charge. The coup was almost complete.

Soviet army tanks lined Red Square and other key positions in Moscow during the coup of August 1991.

But the State Emergency Committee had made one big blunder. They had not arrested the second most powerful man in the land—Boris Yeltsin. Gorbachev may have been the head of the Soviet

12

Union, but Yeltsin had recently been elected as the first official president of Russia, which was aiming to regain its own separate identity, free of Communist control. The election of the tough, flamboyant Yeltsin meant that there were two men ruling the same country.

Gorbachev and Yeltsin were rivals and did not like one another. But on this historic day, they were on the same side—the side of progress and openness for the Russian people against the forces of dictatorship and repression. Gorbachev was a prisoner, but Yeltsin was still free.

That morning, Yeltsin's daughter had woken him early in his home on the outskirts of Moscow. She told him about the coup, and he learned that Gorbachev was under arrest. He dressed quickly, put on a bulletproof vest, and drove to the center of the city. His destination was the White House, home of the Russian parliament and now the center of resistance to the State Emergency Committee. This, too, was surrounded by army tanks. The troops and vehicles were there to show the strength of the armed forces and as a threat to Parliament.

Yeltsin did not hesitate. As he strode past the tanks and into the White House, he was determined to stand up against the plotters. In Parliament, he declared that the coup was an act of madness and demanded that Gorbachev be released.

By now, the crisis had caught the attention of the Russian people. Thousands gathered outside the Russian White House, forming a human barrier to protect Parliament from the troops. It soon became clear that the army commanders did not know what to do. Some had already decided to change sides and ignore the orders of the State Emergency Committee.

HOW THE SOVIET UNION WAS GOVERNED

Until 1989, the Soviet Union was controlled by the Communist Party. Although there was a parliament called the Supreme Soviet, its job was simply to accept the decisions made by the Communist Party.

The bold response of Yeltsin (holding white paper) to the coup stopped the plotters from taking over the building that housed Parliament.

That afternoon, Yeltsin made a bold move. He climbed on top of a tank and made a defiant speech. He said that the coup was against the law and the plotters were guilty of treason. He was president

of Russia, and he was taking control of all Russian territory. This dramatic moment was watched by television viewers all over the world.

Yeltsin's speech marked the beginning of the end for the State Emergency Committee. Support for Yeltsin and Gorbachev grew rapidly—both in Russia and abroad. On August 20, 1991, the U.S. president, the British prime minister, and other world leaders promised backing for the Russian government. The next day, most of the plotters were arrested. One committed suicide. Mikhail Gorbachev and his family returned to Moscow, shaken but unharmed.

COMMUNIST PARTY STRUCTURE

General Secretary
↓
Politburo
(12–15 members)
↓
Central Committee
(360 members)
↓
Communist Party Congress
(5,000 delegates)
↓
regional party organizations,
called *soviets*
↓
district party organizations
↓
local party organizations (in
factories, collective farms, etc.)

The August Coup was over. But Russia—and the Soviet Union—would never be the same again. The iron grip of the Communist Party had been broken at last. Within a few months, the Soviet Union itself would disappear from the map. ▰

The Communist Triumph

Chapter

2

The Soviet Union had strong beginnings. It was an experiment in a completely new kind of government, based on the theories of communism. This experiment began in 1917, when Russia, then an independent country, was boiling up into revolution. For three centuries, Russians had suffered under the brutal rule of the Romanov dynasty of tsars, or emperors. Most peasants were little better than slaves, and there were severe shortages of food across the land. In 1917, the Russian army was being humiliated by the Germans in World War I. The system wasn't working, and people had had enough.

In March 1917, the revolution came to a climax. Strikes and riots broke out in Petrograd (later called Leningrad and now called St. Petersburg, its original name), and Tsar Nicholas II was forced

to give up the throne. He was later killed. Social unrest swept across the country again that October, and soon a new set of rulers had taken control of the government in Moscow. They were known as the Bolsheviks, a radical group of revolutionaries headed by Vladimir Ilyich Lenin. The revolution became known as the Bolshevik Revolution.

Strikes and riots swept through Moscow and Petrograd at the outbreak of the Russian Revolution of 1917.

17

Vladimir Ilyich Lenin became chairman of the government led by the Bolsheviks after the Russian Revolution of 1917.

Lenin declared that the aim of the Bolsheviks was to establish a communist society. He was convinced that the old capitalist system was about to collapse throughout Europe, Asia, and the United States. He believed there would be a global revolution in which ordinary people would overthrow their leaders, abolish private property, and treat each other as equals. In the end, he said, the whole world would become communist.

The Bolsheviks had to act quickly to stay in power. They withdrew the Russian army from World War I and signed a peace treaty with Germany—even though this meant losing a huge

LENIN

Vladimir Ilyich Lenin (1870–1924) became a revolutionary radical after his brother was executed for trying to murder the tsar. Lenin was sent into exile in the West, but he returned to Russia in 1917 and became leader of the Bolsheviks. After the Russian Revolution of 1917, he established the U.S.S.R. as the world's first communist state, ruling as a ruthless dictator.

amount of territory. They passed laws making private trade illegal and took over large factories, mines, and other parts of industry. Ordinary workers had already formed local *soviets*, or councils, and had begun to seize land and houses from private owners.

However, Lenin realized that the revolution had to be kept on a tight rein. Society would not become free and equal overnight. He believed there first had to be a period of strict state control. This would give time for his government to tear down the old system and build a communist system in its place.

19

In order to gain the control he sought, Lenin set up a secret police force, called the Cheka, to make sure that people obeyed the new laws. Bolsheviks took over all the local soviets. Strikes and demonstrations by workers were ruthlessly crushed by government troops. The troublemakers—and innocent people as well—were executed without any trial. In the end, Bolshevik rule became a dictatorship every bit as harsh as that of the Romanov rulers.

The communist takeover of power alarmed many Russians and horrified other world leaders. This led to a bitter civil war that divided the country and lasted from 1918 to 1921. On one side were the communist Reds, and on the other were the anticommunist Whites. The White Russians were backed by troops from the United States, France, Great Britain, and other countries. The Red army defeated these combined enemies, but the conflict left the Russian people facing widespread famine and industrial chaos.

CAPITALISM AND COMMUNISM

Most countries, including the United States, have a capitalist system. The main aim of capitalism is to build up capital, or money. Factories, land, shops, and other parts of the economy can be privately owned, and people are generally free to have as much property as they like. Russia, and later the Soviet Union, had a communist system, however. In this type of system, the state owns all factories, land, and other parts of the economy. The government plans and controls most aspects of society. German thinker Karl Marx, along with Friedrich Engels, is credited with developing the modern ideas of communism during the 1800s.

Yet victory in the civil war gave the Bolsheviks even greater power. In 1918, the Bolsheviks renamed themselves the All-Russian Communist Party—the only political party allowed to exist in Russia. In 1922, the Union of Soviet Socialist Republics (U.S.S.R), or Soviet Union, was established. At first it consisted of just four republics: Russia, Belorus, Transcaucasia (which included Georgia), and Ukraine. Soon it was joined by three others: Tajikistan, Turkmenistan, and Uzbekistan.

Lenin died in 1924, sparking a long struggle among those who might take his place. It was not until 1929 that Joseph Stalin crushed the last of his rivals to become the new Soviet leader. Stalin was an utterly ruthless man, and he quickly gained complete control of the Communist Party and the Soviet government.

Stalin's most important task was to reshape Russia's industries and farming. He started a series of Five-Year Plans, which laid down targets for every part of the economy. The first Five-Year Plan decreed that heavy industries, such as chemical production, coal mining, and steelmaking, should expand rapidly. The result was that the country doubled its industrial output in a short time.

Stalin was also determined that the state should control the nation's food supply. His plan ordered peasants to give up their own small pieces of land to be combined with others into huge collective farms. The state ran these farms and took

21

Joseph Stalin was dictator of the Soviet Union from 1929 until his death in 1953.

all the crops, which they bought from the peasants at very low prices. Millions who protested were shot or sent to prison labor camps in faraway Siberia, a cold and remote area of Russia.

This was just the start of an appalling campaign of terror unleashed by Stalin. He grew obsessed with stamping out all opposition. He even suspected enemies among his own Communist followers. During the Great Purges of 1934 to 1939, the secret police arrested more than 7 million Soviet citizens, ranging from major politicians to ordinary workers. Most of them died as a result—half by execution and half in labor camps. By 1939, nearly one Russian in 10 was in a prison camp.

Much worse was to come. That same year saw the start of World War II, with the German invasion of much of Western Europe. The Soviet Union had made a pact with Germany, in which both countries promised not to attack each other. This gave Stalin the chance to invade the Baltic nations of Estonia, Latvia, and Lithuania, and add them to the Soviet Union.

Then, in June 1941, the country received a shattering blow. Adolf Hitler, the German leader, broke his agreement with Stalin and sent a vast army to invade the Soviet Union. German tanks and aircraft swept into northwestern Russia, capturing the city of Kiev and attacking the major cities of Leningrad (now St. Petersburg) and Stalingrad (now Volgograd). It seemed that nothing could stop them.

JOSEPH STALIN

Joseph Djugashvili was the son of a poor shoemaker in the country of Georgia. As a young man, he became a Bolshevik revolutionary and took the name of Stalin, which means "man of steel." A brilliant organizer, he became the general secretary of the Communist Party in 1922 and Soviet leader in 1929. Over the next quarter of a century, he ruthlessly killed off or exiled anyone he thought of as a threat. Millions of Soviets died while he was in power, many of them due to his cruel policies. Stalin himself died in 1953.

23

But the Red army fought back stubbornly. They were helped by the bitter cold of the winter of 1942. The freezing temperatures shattered the Germans' resolve, who were by then far from home and running out of supplies. Slowly the Soviet troops drove back the invaders and then surrounded them, forcing a surrender early in 1943.

Soviet soldiers had to cope with bitterly cold conditions during World War II. Some soldiers wore white camouflage uniforms and traveled on skis.

The Red army followed up its triumph by pushing westward through Eastern Europe until

24

it reached Berlin, the German capital. Here the army met the other Allied forces, which had fought their way from the south and west. Berlin fell early in May 1945, and the war in Europe ended in an Allied victory. The Soviet Union had paid a heavy price: As many as 10 million of its soldiers lost their lives, as well as 10 million civilians. This was by far the biggest death toll of all the warring countries.

For all its agony and bloodshed, World War II was very good for Stalin. He ended up on the winning side, and this success and prestige gave him an even tighter grip on power in the Soviet Union. It also made him an equal partner in victory with Great Britain and the United States. This gave him a strong bargaining position when the leaders of the "Big Three" countries met to discuss the future of Europe.

THE SOVIET DEAD 1918–1953

Estimated death tolls of the great Soviet disasters under Lenin and Stalin:

The civil war 1918–1921	10 million
The famines 1921–1922	5 million
The Great Purges 1934–1939	6 million
World War II 1940–1945	20 million

This meeting took place at Potsdam, Germany, in July 1945. Stalin started the talks with a big advantage because the other two leaders were new to their jobs. Harry S. Truman had just become the U.S. president after the death of Franklin D. Roosevelt, and Clement Attlee had recently replaced Winston Churchill as British prime minister.

At the conference, the Allies agreed to divide Germany into four zones. The Soviet Union took the eastern zone. This included Berlin, though the city was also divided into four zones.

Clement Attlee (from left), Harry S. Truman, and Joseph Stalin, the Big Three Allied leaders, met for the first time at Potsdam, Germany, in July 1945.

Each zone was occupied by one of the four Allied powers: Great Britain, France, the United States, and the Soviet Union.

The Soviets also retained a large slice of eastern Poland and gained partial control of Romania, Bulgaria, and Hungary. Stalin promised that he would leave these nations free to choose their own kinds of government. He did not intend to honor these promises, however. His aim was to keep as much of Eastern Europe as possible under tight Soviet control. ◣

Behind the Iron Curtain

Chapter

3

At the end of 1945, the Soviet Union had the biggest army in the world. It had regained much of the territory it lost after World War I. But it was a country in ruins. Railways, factories, mines, and farmlands lay devastated after the long struggle with Germany. At least 20 million of its citizens had died.

Russia had been invaded three times in 150 years. Stalin was determined that this would never happen again. His main objective now was to create a buffer zone along the border with the West, which would protect the Soviet Union against any land attack from that direction. At the same time, he wanted to increase the size and power of his empire by taking firm control of neighboring countries.

After the war, many people tried to leave Soviet-dominated areas. Some refugees fled to West Berlin and stayed in an empty factory building that served as a temporary shelter.

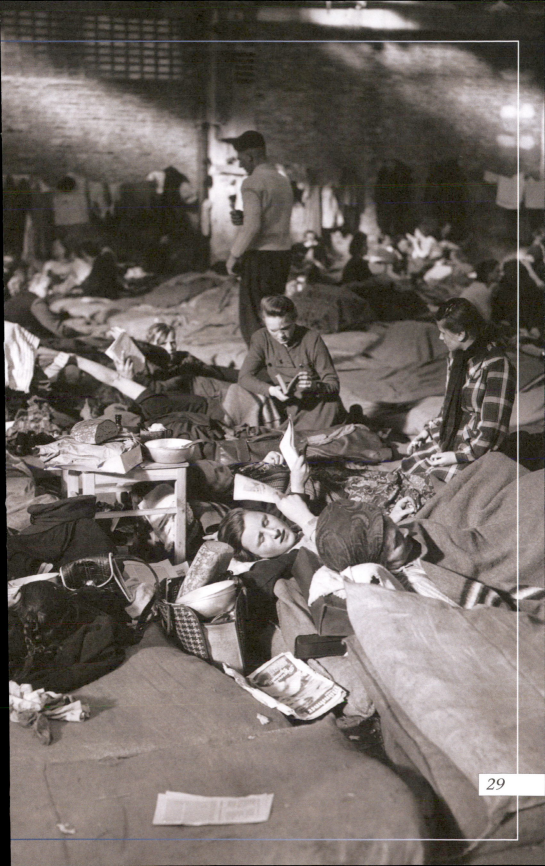

Stalin had promised the other Allied leaders that he would allow free elections in the countries of Eastern Europe that bordered the Soviet Union. But he secretly ordered his agents to establish communist governments in these states. They did this slowly, through a gradual takeover of the police, armed forces, and the economy. Opposing political parties were driven from power and then destroyed.

In this way, Poland, East Germany, Romania, Bulgaria, Albania, Hungary, Yugoslavia, and later Czechoslovakia became satellite states. This meant they were outside the Soviet Union but actually ruled by the Soviet government.

In 1946, British politician Winston Churchill famously described the line that ran through Europe and divided the continent into communist and noncommunist sides:

> An iron curtain has descended across the [European] continent.

DEATH IN PRISON CAMPS

By 1946, labor camps throughout the Soviet Union held more than 10 million Russian men and women—about 10 percent of the entire population of the Soviet Union. This network of prison camps was known as the Gulag. Created by Joseph Stalin in the early 1930s to house anybody accused of being an enemy of the state, the Gulag grew into the biggest system of prisons in history. At least 1 million people died in the Gulag because of harsh conditions, lack of food, and exhausting physical work.

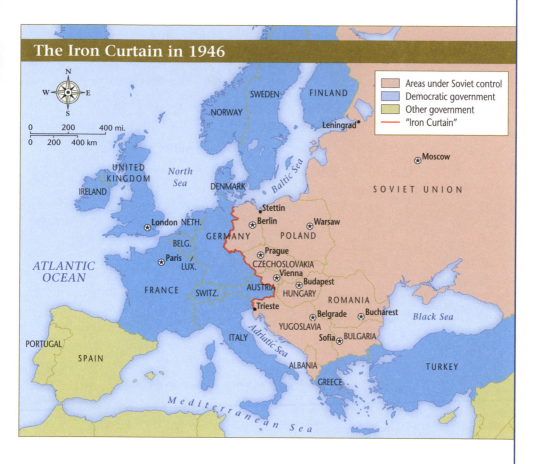

The Iron Curtain in 1946

Areas under Soviet control
Democratic government
Other government
"Iron Curtain"

SWEDEN · FINLAND · NORWAY · Leningrad · Moscow · SOVIET UNION

UNITED KINGDOM · North Sea · DENMARK · Baltic Sea · IRELAND

Stettin · Berlin · Warsaw · London · NETH. · GERMANY · POLAND · BELG. · Prague · Paris · LUX. · CZECHOSLOVAKIA · Vienna · Budapest · FRANCE · SWITZ. · AUSTRIA · HUNGARY · ROMANIA · Trieste · Belgrade · Bucharest · Black Sea · YUGOSLAVIA · ITALY · Sofia · BULGARIA · PORTUGAL · SPAIN · ALBANIA · TURKEY · GREECE

ATLANTIC OCEAN · Adriatic Sea · Mediterranean Sea

0 200 400 mi.
0 200 400 km

The Soviet Union and the United States were without question the leading powers in the world. In fact, they were known as superpowers and were far stronger than any other countries. The United States and Soviet Union had been allies in World War II, but now they were rivals, with each wanting to spread its influence around the world.

Not surprisingly, U.S. and other Western leaders soon grew increasingly alarmed at the Soviets' actions, which were threatening the free countries of Europe.

The Soviet Union and its satellite states occupied much of Eastern Europe.

Stalin was building up a new Soviet empire, pushing communism both westward and southward. The United States countered this in 1947 by giving economic aid to many countries still shattered by the war, such as Greece and Italy. They hoped that stronger nations would be able to stand up to Soviet pressure.

Stalin was suspicious of the United States. After all, the Americans had the most horrifying and powerful weapon in history—the atomic bomb. The first of these bombs, dropped on Hiroshima, Japan, in 1945, had killed 80,000 people in a split second. Clearly, anyone who could build such a devastating device would be able to rule the world. Stalin feared that the United States would use the threat of nuclear strikes to put pressure on him. He ordered his scientists to develop an atomic bomb as quickly as possible.

Success came in August 1949, when the first Soviet atomic bomb exploded on a remote test site in the Soviet republic of Kazakhstan. Now both superpowers had nuclear weapons. This marked the real beginning of what was called the Cold War. The war was "cold" rather than "hot" because the two sides did not fight each other directly in battle. Both Soviets and Americans knew that atomic warfare could wipe out most of the human race, leaving no winners.

Knowing that atomic warfare had no winners did not stop the Soviets and Americans from building up huge stockpiles of nuclear bombs and missiles over the next three decades. In fact, this is in part what kept the war a cold one. The appalling power of such weapons was so great that it stopped the two sides from using them. This was called the deterrent effect. But it only worked if both sides had a roughly equal number of nuclear weapons.

The deterrent effect made it vital that the Soviet Union keep up with the United States in this arms race. In order to so do, the country needed a strong economy and heavy industry. But the Soviet Union started at a huge disadvantage, because the United States had a much healthier economy. Instead of being hurt by the war, U.S. industries were booming. The United States controlled most of the world's production of vital materials such as oil, gas, aluminum, and copper. The Soviet Union lagged far behind.

Stalin was determined to catch up. His series of Five-Year Plans demanded an even more rapid growth in industry. This did not help ordinary

THE BERLIN AIRLIFT

In June 1948, the Soviet army blocked the roads and railways that led to the zones of Berlin occupied by the United States, Great Britain, and France. By blocking the roads, they cut off supplies to more than 2 million people living in those zones. British and U.S. cargo planes brought food and other supplies into the blocked zones. This operation became known as the Berlin Airlift and it lasted until the road blockade ended in May 1949. Although the Cold War did not include any actual battles, this is an example of one of the stand-offs the two countries experienced.

33

By testing the atomic bomb, the Soviet Union showed it had the capability to use nuclear weapons as the United States had used them against Japan in World War II.

citizens. Factories were now focused on producing equipment for the army. Guns, bombs, tanks, and aircraft were manufactured instead of clothes, shoes, toys, and furniture. Wages were still very low, and there was never enough food. The new system of collective farms was proving to be disastrous.

By now, Stalin was a sick man, and he was more suspicious than ever of those around him. He even had his own doctors arrested and tortured because he was convinced they were trying to kill him. In the end, he died of a stroke in March 1953. Once again, there was a long struggle for power among the members of the Politburo, the ruling group in the Communist Party. The eventual winner was Nikita Khrushchev, who took control in 1955 and became official Soviet leader in 1958.

Khrushchev faced huge difficulties. Stalin had dominated and terrified Soviet citizens for nearly 25 years, but now that he was gone, people in the Soviet satellite countries felt free to protest. Workers in East Germany and Poland went on strike. In 1956, Hungary announced that it was going to free itself from Soviet control. Soviet troops and tanks quickly moved in and crushed the uprising, killing thousands of Hungarians.

Khrushchev was also facing problems closer to home. The country's food shortage was an ongoing problem that he made efforts to improve with some success. His solution was simple: Use more land to produce more food. By 1960, nearly 90 million acres (36 million hectares) of new land had been plowed for growing crops. He also created even bigger collective farms by combining the small ones. As a result, agricultural production rose swiftly, though at the same time living conditions for farm workers grew much worse.

Nikita Khrushchev, the Soviet leader from 1955 to 1964, made great efforts to boost Soviet agriculture.

The Soviet Union now entered an era of spectacular success. In 1959, Khrushchev introduced a Seven-Year Plan, which nearly doubled industrial output, especially in oil, gas, and chemicals. Soviet scientists had already astonished the world by putting the first man-made satellite, called *Sputnik,* into orbit in 1957. Three years later, they also sent the first human into space, Yuri Gagarin.

Meanwhile, the Cold War was coming dangerously close to heating up. The U.S.S.R. actively encouraged communists to take over governments in other parts of the world. The United States tried to counter these actions. As future U.S. Secretary of State Henry Kissinger later explained:

> *The two superpowers often behave like two heavily armed blind men feeling their way around a room, each believing himself in mortal peril from the other, whom he assumes to have perfect sight.*

Sometimes, the conflicts blew up into local wars. In the Korean War (1950–1953), the communist North attacked the democratic and capitalist South. The United States and other Western countries believed the Soviet Union was backing North Korea, and sent troops to defend South Korea. More than 3 million people died during this conflict. Similarly, in the Vietnam War (1959–1975), communist forces from the North

The U.S. Army trained many soldiers from South Vietnam to fight in the war against the communist North.

tried to overthrow the government in the South. The Soviet Union supported the North Vietnamese, while the United States and 40 other countries supported the South Vietnamese.

In 1961, the East German government, backed by the Soviets, built a high wall blocking off their section of Berlin. Made of concrete and barbed wire, the Berlin Wall was a visible symbol of the Iron Curtain, the line that divided the communist world from the West.

By the late 1960s, it was clear to both sides in the Cold War that they had to do something to control the nuclear arms race. The Strategic Arms Limitation Talks (SALT) began in 1969 between the Soviet Union's new leader, Leonid Brezhnev, and U.S. President Richard M. Nixon. A second round of SALT meetings in 1974 ended with both sides agreeing to limit their stores of weapons. This was the start of a period of friendlier relations between East and West. But how long would it last? ◣

THE CUBAN MISSILE CRISIS

The nearest the world came to nuclear war was during the Cuban Missile Crisis of 1962. The United States found evidence that Soviet missiles with nuclear warheads had been shipped to Cuba, only 90 miles (144 km) from the Florida coast. U.S. President John F. Kennedy threatened to go to war unless they were removed. After 13 days of frightening suspense, Khrushchev agreed to withdraw the weapons.

Enter Gorbachev

The thaw in the Cold War did not last long. Even while apparently having friendly relations with other nations, the Soviet Union went on producing weapons. By 1976, it had a stockpile of nuclear arms as big as that of the United States. Each nation now had enough long-range missiles and other hardware to destroy the other several times over. No one could possibly win. The Americans called this situation "mutual assured destruction," or MAD for short. It was clear proof that neither side trusted the other.

In the end, the arms race helped to destroy the Soviet Union. Its giant army required a vast amount of money for training, equipment, and wages. A large part of heavy industry and scientific research was taken up with fulfilling the needs of the armed forces. This meant that there was little money left for producing consumer goods or for building up the country's roads, railways, and other services.

The Soviet Union, with all its terrifying military strength, looked to the rest of the world like a mighty fortress that would stand forever. But inside, it was rotting away. The original ideals of the Russian Revolution of 1917 had almost entirely disappeared. All the Soviet leaders seemed to care about was defying the United States abroad and maintaining absolute power at home. The great communist experiment in fairness and equality had turned into one of the cruelest dictatorships in history.

Every year on May 1, the Soviet Union showed off its military might with a parade of weapons, troops, and images of Lenin in Moscow's Red Square.

Leonid Brezhnev, who had replaced the fiery Khrushchev as leader in 1964, had begun his political career during the Stalin years. A modest and quiet man, he had no intention of reforming Soviet society. He did little to relax the strict state control of most aspects of life and stamped fiercely on any kind of protest movement. There was no such thing as free speech.

Leonid Brezhnev was the Soviet leader from 1964 until his death in 1982. In his later years, he was sick and barely able to make decisions.

By the mid-1970s, at least 10,000 people were still being held in prisons and camps throughout the country. These included many Jews and Christians who defied Communist Party rules to openly practice their religion. Writers, artists, and scientists who had criticized the Soviet regime were also held. Most lived in harsh conditions, half-starved and forced to do hard labor. The most dedicated dissidents, or protesters, were labeled insane and locked up in mental asylums.

The Soviet leaders were quick to crush any opposition, whether it came from within the U.S.S.R. or from its Eastern European satellites. In 1968, Soviet troops invaded Czechoslovakia when the government there started a reform program. During the 1970s, people in the Soviet republics of Ukraine and Georgia and in the Baltic republics demanded more freedom from Soviet control. Brezhnev would not allow this, but the nationalist movements kept growing. In 1977, Armenian nationalists exploded a bomb on the Moscow subway, and widespread strikes began in Poland.

A much greater disaster was about to unfold. In late 1979, the Soviet Union invaded Afghanistan in an attempt to strengthen the communist government there. But the massive Soviet army of 100,000 men, with all of its modern weapons, was unable to defeat the poorly armed Afghan resistance fighters. Over the next three years, more than 5,000 Soviet soldiers and airmen lost their lives in this futile conflict.

43

Soviet troops and tanks invaded Afghanistan on December 25,1979. It was the start of a long nightmare.

The war in Afghanistan outraged the rest of the world. Many countries refused to attend the 1980 Summer Olympic Games, which were held in Moscow. The U.S. government broke off trade agreements with the Soviet Union, which included the selling of much-needed grain. The United States also supplied arms and money to the Afghan guerrillas, who were soon joined by volunteers from all parts of the Islamic world.

The Soviet government had by this time reached a standstill. The average age of Politburo members was 69, and these men were not prepared to make any tough decisions, let alone introduce any reforms. Its meetings were almost a joke. Brezhnev was ill, drugged, and sometimes drunk. Few could hear what he said. Brezhnev died in November 1982, and was replaced by Yuri Andropov.

THE SOVIETS CATCH UP

Comparative production figures for the superpowers in 1980 (in tons/metric tons):

	U.S.S.R.	U.S.
Coal	501 million (451 million)	566 million (509.5 million)
Petroleum	572 million (515 million)	429 million (386 million)
Meat	12.5 million (11 million)	17 million (15 million)
Wheat	98 million (88 million)	64 million (57.5 million)
Barley	44.5 million (40 million)	8 million (7 million)

The United States also had a new president, Ronald Reagan, who took a harder line with the Soviet Union than had his predecessor, Jimmy Carter. He warned Soviet leaders that he was ready to back out of the SALT agreements if they did not stop building nuclear weapons. At the same time, the Americans themselves started a colossal new program of arms production. In a speech in Florida in March 1983, Reagan called the Soviet Union "an evil empire" and "the focus of evil in the modern world."

Two weeks later, Reagan revealed that the United States was developing an entirely new kind of weapon. He declared that North America would be covered by an electronic shield in space. This shield would detect enemy missiles and shoot them down with laser beams. Named the Strategic Defense Initiative (SDI), the program was popularly known as the "Star Wars" system.

Former film actor Ronald Reagan was U.S. president from 1981 to 1989. He strongly opposed Soviet influence throughout the world.

Although no one knew if the SDI would actually work, news of the program shocked Soviet leaders. They realized that their country had lost the arms race. The Soviet Union simply did not have the resources to develop weapons that could outwit the SDI, which in the end never went into operation. Andropov was a forward-looking leader, eager to start reforms and to forge warmer relations with the United States. He began new talks with President Reagan on limiting nuclear missile numbers in Europe. At home, he introduced campaigns against corrupt officials, inefficient working methods, and heavy drinking.

However, little came of these projects. Andropov, like Brezhnev, was old and sick and soon unable to attend government meetings. When he died early in 1984, Politburo members had to make their choice of new leadership from two very different men: Konstantin Chernenko, who was 73 years old, crippled with asthma, and out of touch, and Mikhail Gorbachev, who was 53, healthy, and forward-looking. They chose Chernenko.

Gorbachev, who had been Andropov's deputy as Communist Party leader, waited patiently. He made several state visits abroad, where he impressed everyone with his intelligence and sense of humor. On a trip to Great Britain that year, he charmed the forceful British Prime Minister Margaret Thatcher. "I like Mr. Gorbachev," she said. "We can do business together." His growing international fame, not surprisingly, made other Politburo members jealous.

However, they were too late to stop Gorbachev's rise to power, for he was just as popular inside the Soviet Union. When Chernenko died a year later— in March 1985—the Politburo quickly decided to appoint Gorbachev as the new general secretary, or leader, of the Communist Party. After being offered the position, Gorbachev told his wife, Raisa:

> *I have come here with hope and the belief that I shall be able to accomplish something. Therefore, if I really want to change something, I have to accept the nomination. … We can't go on living like this.*

He declared that the Soviet Union had to make progress by developing its science and technology and by creating a more just society. He promised that the state would operate with greater *glasnost*, a Russian word that means "openness" or "frankness."

Gorbachev was determined to make major reforms to the Soviet system. But he knew that he could not achieve this unless he first reformed the Politburo itself. Quietly, he got rid of the old guard from

Gorbachev's popularity was helped by his wife, Raisa, who was far more glamorous and lively than any previous Soviet leader's wife.

MIKHAIL GORBACHEV

Mikhail Gorbachev was born in Stavropol, in southern Russia, in 1931. He worked on the local collective farm before going to Moscow State University. Intelligent, energetic, and ambitious, he secretly scorned the ignorant and greedy Communist Party bosses he met. All the same, Gorbachev was a dedicated party member, joining the Central Committee in 1971 and the Politburo in 1980. There he became an ally and friend of Yuri Andropov.

48

the Brezhnev era and replaced them with younger and more dynamic politicians. Over the next year, more than half of all senior government officials were replaced.

The policy of glasnost brought many surprises. Gorbachev made regular visits to towns and factories, mixing with ordinary workers and listening to what they had to say. His wife, Raisa, often went with him. He made public speeches without notes. He gave interviews to foreign journalists, including one for *Time* magazine. No Soviet leader had ever acted so frankly and openly before. It was the beginning of a massive change in the politics of the Soviet Union—a change that would ultimately destroy the country. ◣

The Fall of the Iron Curtain

Chapter 5

When Mikhail Gorbachev came to power, the Soviet economy was in a terrible state. This was largely due to the Cold War, which continued to eat up huge amounts of money. The Soviet Union spent as much as 50 percent of its yearly budget on weapons and the armed forces. And every year, about $3 billion went to support other communist countries.

Gorbachev knew that his reforms would fail if he could not find an end to the arms race. In November 1985, he had his first summit meeting with Ronald Reagan. It did not start well. After their first discussion, Gorbachev described the U.S. president as "a cave man, a political dinosaur." However, the two men soon warmed to each other.

Gorbachev and Reagan had a second summit meeting a year later in Reykjavik, Iceland. This led to an agreement between the two superpowers to get rid of some of their smaller nuclear missiles. At the same time, Gorbachev took the first steps to end the ongoing disaster in Afghanistan by calling home 6,000 Soviet troops. He also drew up plans to recall the remaining 90,000 soldiers within the next three years.

Then, a national disaster showed just how dangerous and inefficient the Soviet system had become. On April 26, 1986, the nuclear power plant at Chernobyl in Ukraine blew up after a mistake by its operators. Thirty-one people were killed and

U.S. President Ronald Reagan (left) and Soviet General Secretary Mikhail Gorbachev met for their first summit in Geneva, Switzerland.

more than 500 injured in the explosion. But this was just the beginning of the tragedy. The blast sent clouds of deadly radioactive dust high into the air. Within weeks, the dust had reached many other countries in Europe, poisoning land, crops, and animals. This disaster shocked the world. The effects of the radiation are still killing people in the Chernobyl area to this day.

The disastrous explosion at the Chernobyl nuclear power station damaged the reputation of the Soviet Union worldwide.

During this time, Gorbachev increased his efforts to give the Soviet economy a new structure. He called this policy *perestroika*, which means "rebuilding" in Russian. For decades, industry had been completely controlled by the state in its rigid Five-Year Plans.

Gorbachev tried to reduce the government's role in managing the economy, letting it operate more freely. The market itself would dictate what products should be made and how expensive they should be. This was the Western, capitalist way of running things.

The related policy of glasnost also affected the economy. Gorbachev was eager to take notice of the human element in industry, which meant listening to what ordinary workers wanted and how they were treated. This new freedom extended to many other areas of society, too. Censorship rules were relaxed, and writers and journalists were encouraged to discuss how they saw the Soviet future. Foreign radio stations, such as the Voice of America and the British Broadcasting Company were given official permission to broadcast in the Soviet Union.

In 1988, Gorbachev made another significant break with the past. He announced that a special commission had cleared the names of many people who had been executed under Stalin. Newspapers were instructed to make harsh criticisms of Stalin and his rule. In 1990, the

Soviet government admitted that it had been responsible for the murders of thousands of Polish officers during World War II. For the first time, the Soviet Union was accepting the blame for its past atrocities.

This was an amazing transformation, but it spelled trouble for Gorbachev. His liberal reforms had started to loosen the chains of dictatorship and state control that had bound the Soviet people for so long. This created trouble from two sides. On one side were the Communist Party conservatives. They were shocked to see the old policies being changed and power being taken away from the Communist Party. These conservatives still thought of Stalin as a great leader and refused to believe that he was a murderous monster. They spoke bitterly against Gorbachev's measures at the 1987 Communist Party Congress.

On the other side were the liberals. They thought that Gorbachev was moving too slowly and cautiously. Many Soviet citizens now felt bold enough to criticize him. They had hoped for great changes but found that rebuilding the economy had not actually improved their working and living conditions.

One of Gorbachev's fiercest critics was Boris Yeltsin, who had joined the Politburo in 1985. Fiery and often rude, Yeltsin complained that perestroika was moving too slowly. He argued that Gorbachev's promises were empty and that his colleagues were corrupt bullies. At first, Gorbachev tried to protect Yeltsin, but by late 1987, he had grown irritated with Yeltsin's constant criticism of his policies. He forced Yeltsin to resign, telling him, "I will never allow you back into big-time politics."

Little did Gorbachev know that he had made a powerful enemy. All the same, these attacks from

Gorbachev appointed Boris Yeltsin to the Politburo in 1985. Yeltsin later became the president of Russia.

both sides astonished and upset Gorbachev. He had never wanted to harm the Soviet Union and had no grand plan to break it apart. He was a faithful member of the Communist Party who still believed in the revolutionary ideals of Lenin. Gorbachev's intention was to reform the Communist Party from within and make it stronger for the future.

BORIS YELTSIN

Boris Yeltsin was a key figure in the breakup of the Soviet Union. Born in 1931 to poor peasant parents in central Russia, he worked as a builder and was a dynamic member of the Communist Party. In 1985, he became a member of the Politboro in Moscow, but after continued criticism of the Soviet leader, he was forced to resign. Yeltsin left the Communist Party in 1990 and a year later was elected president of Russia. Dogged by bad health, he gave up the post in 1999.

The next step in Gorbachev's reform process came in June 1988. He announced at the Communist Party Conference that in the future, the Soviet Union would be ruled by a single president and a Congress of People's Deputies. This would replace the Supreme Soviet, the old Soviet parliament, which had no real power in government. The Soviet people would choose these deputies in free elections. Until now, there had only been one political party in elections— the Communist Party. Now there would be open competition. As Gorbachev had explained to the Communist Party Congress in 1987:

The political system is being radically transformed. True democracy with free elections, a multi-party system, and human rights are being established and genuine government by the people is being reborn. … The U.S.S.R. has become a nation open to the world and co-operation, one that does not evoke fear, but rather commands respect and solidarity.

The first free election took place in January 1989. The Communist Party did well, winning 85 percent of the seats in the Congress of People's Deputies. But the crucial fact was that rival parties also had members elected. This was the end of one-party rule in the Soviet Union after more than 70 years.

Gorbachev was delighted at the success of his reforms. But trouble was looming. He did not realize that once the process of change had started it would be impossible to stop. He also failed to recognize an even more powerful force: the nationalist feeling of the republics and satellite states. The communist world had started to crack wide open.

In 1989, there was unrest throughout the Soviet Union. That April, protesters demanded independence from the central government in Moscow. In July, the miners of the Kuzbass coalfield in Siberia went on strike in support of better wages and conditions. Within weeks, the strike had spread across Russia to Ukraine.

In August, 2 million people in the Baltic republics of Estonia, Latvia, and Lithuania joined

in a mass demonstration protesting Soviet rule. There were street rallies in Moldova and Ukraine, where people also called for independence.

Things were just as bad in Eastern Europe. The Communist Party was being thrown from power everywhere. Poland decided to hold

The coal miners of the Kuzbass region of Siberia went on strike for better wages in April 1989. The strike spread quickly across Russia.

free elections. Hungary began to take down the wire fences on its border with Austria. This was truly the first break in the Iron Curtain. It allowed refugees from the communist states of Eastern Europe to cross Hungary and reach the West.

59

The East German government was outraged by this break in the borders and appealed to Moscow for help. Gorbachev refused to send Soviet troops to stop the refugees because he knew that this would harm relations with the West. The decision not to use force was to play a vital role in the collapse of the Soviet Union.

On November 9, the East German leaders gave up and resigned. It was announced that the border between East and West Germany would be reopened. The next morning, the guards opened the gates in the Berlin Wall, and thousands of people joyfully flooded through. Suddenly, the Iron Curtain had been torn in two. West Berliners cheered the people from the East. Families who had been kept apart by the wall were reunited. Strangers hugged each other in sheer happiness. Over the next few weeks, Berliners attacked the hated wall and smashed it to pieces. Within a year, it had almost completely disappeared.

This was just the beginning. The movement for freedom roared on through Eastern Europe. In November 1989, Todor Zhivkov was swept from power after 35 years as the leader of Bulgaria. Communist Party rule in the country ended altogether a few months later. Meanwhile, more than 350,000 protesters were marching through Prague, the capital of Czechoslovakia. Their pressure forced the ruling Communist Party committee to resign. In December, the last of the old communist regimes in Eastern Europe

also collapsed. The brutal dictator of Romania, Nikolai Ceaucescu, was forced from office and executed by firing squad. By the new year of 1990, the communist empire of Eastern Europe had all but disappeared. The Iron Curtain had fallen.

When the Berlin Wall fell in November 1989, many people hacked off pieces of it to take away as souvenirs.

61

Breaking Up

Chapter

6

Now, Gorbachev believed, the Soviet Union could rebuild its own place in the world without having to support other countries. In March 1990, Gorbachev, who up until this point had remained general secretary of the Communist Party, was elected president of the Soviet Union. He had more wide-ranging powers than ever.

However, the Soviet Union was in turmoil and starting to shake itself to pieces. The year had begun with one republic, Azerbaijan, declaring war on another, Armenia, over ethnic differences. There were nationalist riots in Tajikistan. Then came the first free elections in Lithuania, in which the Communist Party lost power. The Lithuanians declared that they were going to break away from the Soviet Union.

Nationalist campaigners in Azerbaijan demonstrated for independence in 1990.

Gorbachev tried severe tactics to keep control. He cut off oil supplies to Lithuania and sent tanks and troops to impose order in the capital, Vilnius. But in the end, he did not want to use force, and the soldiers withdrew. The success of Lithuania's break from the Soviet Union inspired the other Baltic states. On May 4, Latvia declared itself

When Gorbachev cut off Lithuania's oil supplies, there were long lines at filling stations throughout the republic.

64

an independent country, followed soon afterward by Estonia.

The Soviet leadership had actually encouraged this process—by accident. They had allowed each republic to elect its own Congress of Deputies. This gave them more power and made them feel separate from the Soviet Union. Each nation had its own pride and was eager to be out from under the Soviet government's control.

Even Russia, the biggest republic of all, wanted self-rule. In May 1990, its own congress elected a new chairman. They ignored the official candidate and chose instead a man who had been fired from the Politburo and had resigned from the Communist Party: Boris Yeltsin. Yeltsin was jubilant. He said:

> *We haven't just seized an office, we have seized the whole of Russia!*

In June, Russia also declared itself independent. Despite these growing storms, Gorbachev was still full of hope for the future. At that year's Communist Party Conference, he declared that the country was moving away from state control and toward self-government by the people. The Communist Party itself would be reformed. It would become a tolerant, popular party that recognized that communist bodies in the other republics could think for themselves—within strict limits.

But many wondered if this policy would work. It was clear that Gorbachev was being left behind by the speed of events. He had given people more freedom, but he could not provide jobs or opportunities. There were still major shortages of goods in the shops, and even bread was hard to find. The leader's popularity was falling fast, and many people called for him to resign. In November, he was even shot at during a parade in Moscow, though he was unhurt.

By the beginning of 1991, the conflict between the Soviet Union and Russia was coming to a climax. So was the rivalry between Mikhail Gorbachev and Boris Yeltsin. The Baltic republics had now separated themselves from the Soviet Union and were soon followed by Belarus and Georgia. Yeltsin openly encouraged this split. He organized mass demonstrations in Moscow, calling for bigger reforms.

Next, Yeltsin demanded that Russia have its own president. Gorbachev was powerless to refuse. Soon, the Russian people had elected Yeltsin as their first leader. Now there were really two leaders of Russia, ruling almost the same territory from rival bases in Moscow. The big difference was that Yeltsin had a huge amount of popular support.

Gorbachev made desperate efforts to keep the Soviet Union in one piece. He saved money by cutting the military budget. He signed a new

treaty with the United States that reduced the number of nuclear missiles on both sides. He also tried to organize a cash loan from the United States to help the crumbling Soviet economy. Finally, he drew up a new plan for the structure of the Soviet Union itself. The old U.S.S.R. would disappear to be replaced by a looser Union of Sovereign States. This would be made up of Russia plus nine smaller republics.

By the summer of 1991, Russia had two leaders. Gorbachev (right) was still the Soviet president, but Yeltsin had been elected president of Russia.

67

For the old-style Communist Party conservatives, this was going too far. When Gorbachev flew off for a vacation to the Black Sea on August 5, 1991, a group of them finalized their plans to get rid of him. They wanted to see the Communist Party back in power and the Soviet Union put back together again.

But the coup failed. Gorbachev, imprisoned in his dacha, refused to give in to the demands of the State Emergency Committee. Boris Yeltsin rallied popular support in Moscow against the plotters. In spite of the coup's failures, however, the episode spelled the end for Mikhail Gorbachev.

When Gorbachev later flew back to Moscow, on August 22, he knew things had changed completely. He told reporters:

> *I have come back to a different country, and I myself am a different man now.*

He tried to take command again, but his authority had disappeared. The real leader was Boris Yeltsin, who had become a public hero for his stand against the plotters.

RELIGIOUS FREEDOM

Since the revolution in 1917, Bolshevik and then Soviet leaders had tried to stamp out religion and limit all forms of worship. But in October 1990, the Supreme Soviet passed a law allowing complete religious freedom. Christian services were held in St. Basil's Cathedral in Moscow and other Russian churches for the first time since 1918. Dozens of new Islamic mosques were built in the Muslim areas of the Central Asian Republics.

Gorbachev held a press conference when he returned to Moscow after the failed coup. He still seemed confused by his experience.

This was also the end for the Communist Party in the Soviet Union. Vast crowds marched on the party headquarters in Moscow. They were angry with the senior officials who had been behind the coup. On August 24, Gorbachev resigned as head of the Communist Party. He dissolved the Central Committee, the country's ruling body, and within a few days, communist activity had stopped throughout the U.S.S.R.

69

Without the Communist Party, the Soviet Union was dead. Almost immediately, three of the republics in Central Asia—Azerbaijan, Uzbekistan, and Kirghizstan—declared their independence. Others followed in the final months of 1991. But out of the ashes rose a new and more liberal organization, called the Commonwealth of Independent States. The founding members were Russia, Belarus, and Ukraine. They were soon joined by eight other republics, including Moldova, Armenia, Tajikistan, and Uzbekistan.

The official end of the U.S.S.R. came on December 25, 1991. Gorbachev appeared on television and announced that he had resigned as president of the Soviet Union. He said:

> *The policy of dismembering this country is something I cannot subscribe to.*

The man who had started the reforms was eventually destroyed by them. By December 27, 1991, Yeltsin had forced Gorbachev out of his residence at the Kremlin and his office.

As the year ended, the Soviet flag, with its gold hammer and sickle, was lowered for the last time over the Kremlin in Moscow. In its place was raised the white, blue, and red flag of Russia. A new chapter of world history had begun.

The deadly confrontation between the two great superpowers was over. Much of the credit

The red flag had been the symbol of the Soviet Union since the revolution.

for this went to Mikhail Gorbachev. He had started reform at home and had pushed forward plans for ending the arms race. He had even allowed communist rule in Eastern Europe to disappear peacefully. The result was the end of the Soviet empire.

Russia After Communism

Chapter

7

The breakup of the Soviet Union changed the world map and ended the Cold War. But it left its former republics with many of the same old problems. In some ways the problems appeared even worse, because they could no longer be hidden behind the Iron Curtain.

The economy was in shambles. Gorbachev had removed state control of prices and encouraged a free market, but industries and businesses could not change overnight. There were food shortages, which caused people to march and demonstrate their anger in the big cities. Many teachers and other state workers received no wages and pensions for months. The governments simply had no money. Trade was at a standstill, and there was very little money coming in from exports to foreign countries.

After the official breakup of the Soviet Union, the new white, blue, and red flag of Russia was raised above the Kremlin.

THE COLLAPSE OF THE SOVIET UNION

Under the old Soviet system, workers in the republics paid taxes to the Soviet government. Now the republics had to look after themselves, and the amount of tax income going to the Russian government had fallen massively. Worse still, the system for collecting the taxes had broken down.

Russian president Boris Yeltsin had to look abroad for support. On January 8, 1992, barely a week after the U.S.S.R. had disappeared, the newly created European Union (EU) handed over $263 million worth of food aid. Soon afterward, the situation grew so desperate that the United States, Canada, and the EU also began airlifting food supplies to many of the former Soviet republics. Early in 1993, the world's leading industrial nations gave another $3 billion in aid to the Commonwealth of Independent States, while the United States added another $1.6 billion.

Old-style Communists in Russia were outraged. They believed that begging for foreign money was shameful. The collapse of the Soviet Union had brought nothing but chaos and hardship, they said, and they blamed all of the problems on the reform programs of Mikhail Gorbachev and

THE SOVIET DEBT

By 1998, Russia owed a lot of money to other countries: $40 billion. Most of this debt had been built up during the Soviet era. At the same time, other countries owed Russia a lot of money: $70 billion. These were mostly poor nations such as Nicaragua, Vietnam, Angola, and Yemen. Soviet leaders had lent them cash in an attempt to boost communism in those countries, despite the fact that it was never likely to be repaid.

74

Boris Yeltsin. These conservatives believed the only solution to the problems Russia was facing was to return to the strict regime of the hard-line communist era before 1985, when the state controlled everything.

Thousands of Russians marched to protest food shortages, carrying a banner with images of communist thinkers Marx, Engels, and Lenin.

As opposition grew, Yeltsin found that he could not push his new laws through the Russian parliament. On September 21, 1993, Yeltsin took the drastic step of dissolving Parliament, with the promise of new elections before Christmas. But many of the members refused to leave the White House. They sat tight and voted to take away Yeltsin's powers.

Yeltsin responded by cutting off all electricity and other outside links to the building. He then surrounded the building with troops. The Communist members were trapped inside. This was an amazing situation—the exact opposite of what had happened during the August Coup of 1991. Now Yeltsin was the man attacking the White House. After two weeks, he ordered gunners to shell the building and sent commandos to break in. More than 140 people were killed in the battle before the members of Parliament who had remained in the building finally surrendered.

Yeltsin had shown Parliament—and the country—who was in charge. Now he kept his promise and held elections for a new parliament, which would be called the Federal Assembly. Election results showed that the Russian people were still not happy with Yeltsin. Only 70 members of the new assembly were from his party, Russia's Choice. The Communists captured 103 seats, and the Liberals took 64. Still, this was the first truly democratic election in Russia since 1918.

Russia was not the only part of the old U.S.S.R. to face huge problems. The other former republics now had to build up their own economies without outisde support. Many of these states had been split by violence.

When Communist hardliners refused to leave Parliament in late 1993, Yeltsin ordered tanks to shell the building.

Fighting between different ethnic groups in Armenia and Azerbaijan had left hundreds dead. There were also many deaths during a nationalist revolt and civil war in Georgia.

Nationalism caused even more bloodshed inside Russia. The small state of Chechnya in the southwest had declared its independence along with many other republics in 1991. The government had taken little notice at the time, but by 1994, Chechnya was causing a lot of trouble. It had become a haven for criminal gangs and terrorists who operated inside Russia. The Chechen leaders defied Russia's attempts to control them and announced plans to separate from Russia.

Once again, Yeltsin acted tough. Encouraged by his military commanders, he decided to forcibly restore order. In December 1994, Russian warplanes bombed the Chechen capital, Grozny. The bombings were followed by an invasion force of troops, but the Chechens refused to give in. The war dragged on into 1996 before both sides agreed to peace. By that time, more than 50,000 people had been killed and 200,000 refugees had fled the country.

Meanwhile, the reform program was grinding to a halt. In July 1996, Yeltsin won an election to become the first democratically chosen president of Russia, but in the months after his election, his popularity began to fade. He was a sick man, and his policies were doing little to improve the lives of ordinary people.

There was a huge rise in crime, sparked by highly organized criminal gangs who murdered

After several years of the savage Russian campaign in Chechnya, the streets of the capital Grozny lay ruined and deserted.

each other in the streets. State-run industries, such as oil, were sold to private companies, which simply stole the assets and took the money abroad. Russian businessmen were seen as the most corrupt in the world. To cap it all off, statistics published in 1997 showed that the average life expectancy of a Russian person had actually fallen since the collapse of the Soviet system.

ALEXANDER SOLZHENITSYN

The end of communist power also saw the return of exiled celebrities. Russian writer Alexander Solzhenitsyn (1918–) was exiled from his homeland in 1974 and lived in the United States for many years. Imprisoned for eight years under Stalin, he published many books that criticized the Soviet system. These included *The Gulag Archipelago*, a study of the Russian labor camps. In 1994, he arrived back in Russia to a hero's welcome.

Yeltsin had little answer to this. In fact, he was now too sick to run the government properly and was getting ready to retire. In August 1999, Yeltsin fired the prime minister and appointed Vladimir Putin in his place. Later that year, Yeltsin resigned from the presidency and named Putin as his successor.

This was a significant moment. Putin was a quiet and sly politician, a colorless figure who liked to stay in the background. But he also felt strong ties to the old Soviet regime, since he had been an agent in the KGB for many years. At a meeting of Russia's political leaders, he made a point of drinking a toast to the memory of a past dictator— Joseph Stalin.

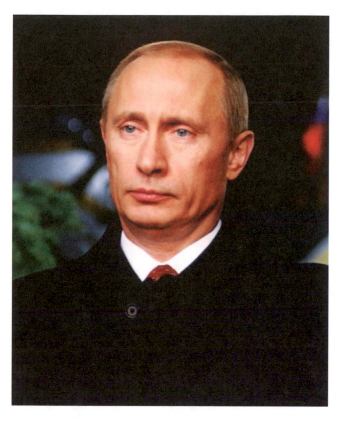

Vladimir Putin became president of Russia in 1999.

Putin believed that the Russian president should have complete control of the country. Within a few months, he had driven out several corrupt businessmen and slapped firmer controls on how newspapers and TV reported current affairs. He also cut back the power of the leaders of the Russian republics and increased government spending on nuclear weapons and the armed forces. ◣

81

The Soviet Collapse and the World

Chapter

8

Vladimir Putin may have respected the memory of Stalin, but Russia was not going back to the dark days of the 1930s purges. The world was now a very different place. For more than 40 years after World War II, the two superpowers of the United States and the Soviet Union had faced each other across the Iron Curtain. The Cold War between them had affected every country in the world and brought the fear of nuclear devastation into every home. Then suddenly, within just a few months, one of those superpowers had vanished. The balance of global politics had shifted dramatically.

It seemed to many that the West had won and a new era of peace and safety had begun. People believed that the end of the Soviet nuclear threat promised a more settled world, free from major

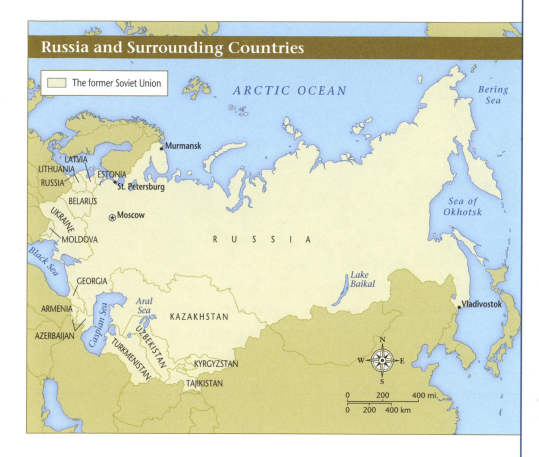

Russia and Surrounding Countries

The former Soviet Union

ARCTIC OCEAN

Bering Sea

Murmansk

LATVIA
LITHUANIA
ESTONIA
RUSSIA
St. Petersburg
BELARUS
Moscow
UKRAINE
MOLDOVA
Black Sea

R U S S I A

Sea of Okhotsk

GEORGIA
ARMENIA
AZERBAIJAN
Caspian Sea
Aral Sea
TURKMENISTAN
UZBEKISTAN
KAZAKHSTAN
KYRGYZSTAN
TAJIKISTAN

Lake Baikal

Vladivostok

N W E S

0   200   400 mi.
0   200   400 km

wars. This new peace would allow economies to grow and bring more prosperity to everyone. But things did not work out so neatly. In fact, in many ways, the collapse of the Soviet Union made international affairs less stable and created a less certain world.

Soviet rule had been harsh, but it had kept a large number of different nations and peoples under control. It had also provided cash and technical support to help their economies. When the republics became independent, they lost most of this.

The collapse of the Soviet Union left Russia and a number of independent states in its place.

83

In a very short time, the new countries had to build up their own ways of running a government and making a living. They also had to learn how to keep their people in order. This could not be done quickly or easily. The result, in some cases, was civil war and bloody conflict between communities of different religious or ethnic backgrounds.

The collapse of the Soviet Union also left a big hole in the structure of world power. From now on, the United States had no major rival to keep it in check. Some people believe that this made the world a more dangerous place because the United States could do exactly what it wanted. There was no longer any real need for the United States to consult anybody else.

Much of St. Petersburg has now been restored to its former glory. Today, the city attracts tourists from all over the world.

However, since 1992, Russia has been slowly rebuilding itself into a major power again.

84

After all, Russia is still the biggest country in the world. It covers one-ninth of Earth's land area, stretching from the Arctic Ocean to the Caucasus Mountains and from the Baltic Sea to the Pacific Ocean. It has the richest store of natural resources of any country in the world. In addition to huge areas of fertile farmland, it contains huge reserves of natural gas, coal, oil, iron, uranium, and other important metals.

Russia is also at the heart of a new group of countries, the Commonwealth of Independent States. The Commonwealth has expanded greatly since it was first established in 1991, and it now includes 11 of the former Soviet republics. These nations work together on economics, defense, and foreign policy. They also aim to use a single currency and even a single language—Russian. Some people have seen the Commonwealth as Russia's way of keeping a hold over its neighboring states.

No matter how powerful Russia becomes, however, the old Soviet Union is gone forever. The Soviet empire had been held together by one thing: the dream of establishing communism throughout the world. But when the empire died, the dream died, too.

For the nations of the West, this dream had been a nightmare that had dominated much of 20th century history. But the collapse of the Soviet Union brought the end of the communist threat. The world today is a freer, safer place. ◣

Timeline

March 1917

Tsar Nicholas II gives up his throne after losing support following a people's revolt.

October 1917

 Revolution takes place in Russia; power passes to the Bolsheviks, headed by V. I. Lenin.

1918-1920

Civil war takes place between Reds (Bolsheviks) and Whites (anti-Bolsheviks); Bolsheviks are victorious.

1922

Union of Soviet Socialist Republics (U.S.S.R.) is established.

1924

Lenin dies; power struggle begins between rival successors.

1929

 Joseph Stalin becomes the new Soviet leader; the first Five-Year Plan for the economy begins.

1934–1939

More than 7 million Russians are arrested in Stalin's purges, and many are executed.

1939

Soviets sign a pact with Germany promising not to invade each other's territory.

1941

German forces invade the U.S.S.R.

1943

German invasion force in the U.S.S.R. surrenders.

1945

 Soviet forces enter Berlin; World War II ends with Allied victory.

1953

Stalin dies; Nikita Khrushchev becomes the Soviet leader.

1961

Soviet cosmonaut Yuri Gagarin becomes the first man in space.

1962

The Cuban Missile Crisis occurs.

1964

Khrushchev is dismissed; Leonid Brezhnev becomes the Soviet leader.

1968

Soviets invade Czechoslovakia.

1974

Second round of SALT talks with the United States leads to an agreement to reduce nuclear arms.

1979

 Soviets invade Afghanistan.

1982

Brezhnev dies; Yuri Andropov becomes the Soviet leader.

1984

Andropov dies and is succeeded by Konstantin Chernenko.

1985

 Chernenko dies; Mikhail Gorbachev becomes the Soviet leader; Gorbachev meets with U.S. President Ronald Reagan.

February 1986

Gorbachev announces the program of perestroika.

April 1986

 Nuclear disaster occurs at Chernobyl.

January 1987

Gorbachev outlines his reform program.

November 1987

Boris Yeltsin is forced to resign from the Central Committee.

April 1988

Treaty is signed to end war in Afghanistan.

December 1988

Gorbachev announces a major cut in the armed forces.

March 1989

Free elections are held for the first Congress of People's Deputies.

May 1989

Estonia and Latvia declare independence.

August 1989

Elections are held in Poland; Communist Party is defeated.

November 1989

The Berlin Wall falls.

February 1990

Free local elections are held in the U.S.S.R.

Timeline

March 1990

Gorbachev is elected president of the U.S.S.R.; Lithuania declares independence.

July/August 1990

Ukraine, Armenia, Turkmenistan, and Tajikistan declare independence.

April 1991

Gorbachev draws up a new treaty for the Soviet Union republics.

June 1991

Yeltsin elected president of Russia.

August 1991

Attempted coup against Gorbachev fails.

August/September 1991

Eleven more republics declare their independence.

December 1991

Gorbachev resigns and announces the end of the Soviet Union.

January 1992

European Union (EU) gives a huge cash loan to Russia.

March 1992

U.S., Canada, and EU airlift food supplies to some former Soviet republics.

September 1993

Yeltsin dissolves the Russian parliament and has face-off with conservatives.

1994–1996

Russian troops fight war in Chechnya.

1999

Yeltsin resigns: Vladimir Putin becomes Russian leader.

HISTORIC SITE

The Cold War Museum
Lorton Nike Missile Base
Route 123 Chain Bridge Road and Interstate 95
Fairfax, VA 22038
703/273-2381

Visitors can view exhibits on the rivalry between the democratic countries of the West and the communist nations of Eastern Europe and Asia

LOOK FOR MORE BOOKS IN THIS SERIES

Hurricane Katrina:
Aftermath of Disaster
ISBN 0-7565-2101-7

Miranda v. Arizona:
The Rights of the Accused
ISBN 0-7565-2008-8

The Little Rock Nine:
Struggle for Integration
ISBN 0-7565-2011-8

The New Deal:
Rebuilding America
ISBN 0-7565-2096-7

McCarthyism:
The Red Scare
ISBN 0-7565-2007-X

Watergate:
Scandal in the White House
ISBN 0-7565-2010-X

A complete list of **Snapshots in History** titles is available on our Web site: *www.compasspointbooks.com*

Glossary

buffer zone
an area of territory between two
rival nations that lessens the danger
of conflict

commando
specially-trained soldiers who make
quick, destructive raids on enemy
territory

conservative
someone who dislikes change and
wants to keep things as they are

coup
sudden action taken to overthrow a
ruler and seize power

democracy
system of government where all people
are allowed to vote freely

deterrent
something that deters or discourages
someone from taking action

dynasty
a succession of rulers from the
same family

economy
the management of money and other
resources by the government of a country

guerrilla
member of a fighting group of
revolutionaries who aim to overthrow
an established government

KGB
Soviet state police force, responsible for
controlling and gathering information

labor camp
prison camp where prisoners are forced
to perform hard manual work

liberal
someone who believes in people's
freedom to act and express themselves
as they wish

nationalism
pride and love of one's native country,
and a strong sense of being part of a
particular national group

pact
a formal agreement or treaty
between nations

Politburo
the "Political Bureau of the Central
Committee" of the Communist Party,
the key decision-making body of the
Soviet Union

purge
the removal of all one's opponents
or possible enemies by force

revolutionary
wanting to bring about major changes
to the government of a country

satellite state
countries controlled by a powerful
neighbor (such as the Soviet Union)

soviet
local council or rule-making body
in revolutionary Russia elected by
the workers

SOURCE NOTES

Chapter 1

Page 11, line 4: Mikhail Gorbachev. *Memoirs*. New York: Doubleday, 1996, p. 815.

Page 12, line 1: David Pryce-Jones. *The War That Never Was: The Fall of the Soviet Empire 1985–1991*. London: Weidenfeld & Nicolson, 1995, p. 409.

Chapter 3

Page 30, line 27: Winston S. Churchill. "Sinews of Peace (Iron Curtain)" Speech. Westminster College, Fulton, Missouri. 5 March 1946. *The Churchill Centre*. 24 Mary 2006. www.winstonchurchill.org/i4a/pages/index.cfm?pageid=429

Page 37, line 17: Henry Kissinger. "The Soviet Riddle." *Time*. 1 Oct. 1979. 24 May 2006. www.time.com/time/archive/preview/0,10987,947453,00.html

Chapter 4

Page 45, line 10: Ronald Reagan. "Remarks at the Annual Convention of the National Association of Evangelicals." 8 March 1983. *American Rhetoric*. 24 May 2006. www.americanrhetoric.com/speeches/ronaldreaganevilempire.htm

Page 47, line 16: Robert Service. *A History of Modern Russia*. London: Penguin, 2003, p. 439.

Page 47, line 27: *Memoirs,* p. 212.

Chapter 5

Page 50, line 14: *A History of Modern Russia*. p. 439.

Page 55, line 4: *Memoirs,* p. 467.

Page 56, line 29: Ibid., p. 313.

SOURCE NOTES

Chapter 6

Page 65, line 17: Boris Yeltsin. *Against the Grain: An Autobiography* (trans. Michael Glenny). London: Jonathan Cape, 1990, p. 365.

Page 68, line 24: *Memoirs,* p. 826.

Page 70, line 16: Ibid.

Select Bibliography

Cipkowski, Peter. *Revolution in Eastern Europe: Understanding the Collapse of Communism in Poland, Hungary, East Germany, Czechoslovakia, Romania, and the Soviet Union.* New York: Wiley, 1991.

Gorbachev, Mikhail. *Memoirs.* New York: Doubleday, 1996.

Head, Tom, ed. *Mikhail Gorbachev.* San Diego: Greenhaven Press, 2003.

Marples, David R. *The Collapse of the Soviet Union: 1985–1991*, Harlow, Eng.: Pearson, 2004.

Pryce-Jones, David. *The War That Never Was: The Fall of the Soviet Empire 1985–1991*. London: Weidenfeld & Nicolson, 1995.

Service, Robert. *A History of Modern Russia.* London: Penguin, 2003.

Strayer, Robert W. *Why Did the Soviet Union Collapse? Understanding Historical Change.* Armonk, N.Y.: M.E. Sharpe, 1998.

Yeltsin, Boris. *Against the Grain: An Autobiography* (trans. Michael Glenny). London: Jonathan Cape, 1990.

Further Reading

Dando, William A., Anna R. Carson, and Carol Z. Dando. *Russia.* Philadelphia: Chelsea House Publishers, 2003.

Langley, Andrew. *Mikhail Gorbachev.* Chicago: Heinemann, 2003.

Matthews, John R. *The Rise and Fall of the Soviet Union.* San Diego: Lucent Books, 2000.

Merrell, Kathleen Berton. *Eyewitness: Russia.* New York: Dorling Kindersley, 2000.

Ross, Stewart. *The Collapse of Communism.* Chicago: Heinemann, 2004.

Smith, Brenda. *The Collapse of the Soviet Union.* San Diego: Lucent Books, 1994.

Index

ABOUT THE AUTHOR

Andrew Langley is the author of many history books for children. These include a biography of Mikhail Gorbachev, *The Roman News*, and *A Castle at War*, which was shortlisted for the Times Education Supplement Information Book Award. He lives in Wiltshire, England, with his family and two dogs.

IMAGE CREDITS